Summer Crochet Patterns

Wonderful Tank Tops

Table of Contents

Introduction 3

Chapter 1 – Guide for Crochet Terms and Hooks 5

Chapter 2 – Easy Breezy Summer Tank 8

Chapter 3 – Cool Mesh Tank 10

Chapter 4 – Easy Tunic Tank 12

Chapter 5 – Sweet Shell Stitch Tank 18

Conclusion 23

Introduction

Crochet tank tops are the best summer time essential for a stylish, cool, and comfortable wardrobe. Why search through racks of clothes, or online stores for the perfect crochet tank top when you can make one yourself? It is cheaper than buying one and you can personalize it for a unique look.

Crochet is a popular fashion trend and these tank tops are will show off that summer tan. Each tank can be customized to fit most sizes with a few stitch changes. Now you can fill your closet with a rainbow of colorful crochet tanks for summer without breaking the bank.

If you are an avid crochet hooker you will have no problem finishing one or more of these tanks in one day. A few hours are all it takes to hook up one of these adorable tops. The patterns show step by step how each tank top is worked up. If you are experienced with crochet you can play with yarn weights and hook sizes to customize the look of each tank.

Crochet tank tops travel easy, they don't wrinkle and washing only makes them softer! They look great over a basic tank, or paired with your favorite bikini. They are so easy to customize with crochet accents you will never need to buy another crochet tank again!

Depending on your skill level, you can add shell stitches to add a bit of lacy flair, or a band of crochet ribbing and make the tank a crop top. A few crocheted flowers and maybe some crochetcd tassels will add some boho style, or you can just loose a few rows of stitches at the bottom and add some fringe for a Woodstock revisited look everyone will love.

These summertime wardrobe wonders are perfect for throwing over a bathing suit when it's time to leave the beach for the board walk. You can make them in colors to match all the bottoms in your wardrobe and still have enough money left over for ice cream. They are great gifts too; everyone loves crochet tank tops because they look great without a lot of effort.

It is easy to change the tank top into a tank dress. Just repeat the last few rows of the tank top and increase a few times until it reaches the length you want. From here you can add patch pockets, crochet accents, or even some fringe and beads.

These patterns will keep you crocheting all summer long and keep your wardrobe looking fresh all season. Each tank is easy to do as long as you know the basic crochet stitches, that's it, no struggling with charts or long abbreviations. Now its time to get started and crochet some hot summer looks.

Chapter 1 – Guide for Crochet Terms and Hooks

Before you begin, look over this chapter to familiarize yourself with the abbreviations used in this book. The abbreviations are standard crochet terms, if you do not know the stitches covered in the abbreviations, it is easy to find an online tutorial for beginners.

If you are already familiar with the stitches listed in the abbreviation chart, you will have no problem crocheting the tank tops in this book. The patterns for each tank use these abbreviations and hook sizes. If you are unfamiliar with these abbreviations, there are many good crochet stitch tutorials online to help you.

Crochet Abbreviations

beg – Beginning	bg - Block
cc – Contrast Color	ch – chain
dc – Double Crochet	dec – Decrease
dtr – Double Treble Crochet	hdc – Half Double Crochet
htr – Half Treble Crochet	inc – Increase
rep – Repeat	rnd – Round

sc – Single Crochet	sl st – Slip Stitch
sp(s) – Space(s)	st(s) – Stitch(s)
tog – Together	tr – Treble Crochet
tr tr – Treble Treble Crochet	WS – Wrong Side
yo – Yarn Over	RS – Right Side
( ) – Work instructions within the parentheses as many times as directed	* - Repeat instructions following the single asterisk as directed
** - Repeat instructions within the asterisk as many times as directed	[ ] – Work instructions within the brackets as many times as instructed

Crochet Hook Sizes

U.S.	English	Metric
14	6	0.60
12	5	0.75

10	4	1.00
-	3	1.25
6	2.5	1.50
4	2	1.75
B	14	2.00
C	12	2.50
D	11	3.00
E	9	3.50
F	8	4.00
G	7	4.50
H	6	5.00
I	5	5.50
J	4	6.00
K	2	7.00
-	1/0	8.00
-	2/0	9.00
P	3/0	10.00

Chapter 2 – Easy Breezy Summer Tank

This tank pattern is for beginners, it is easy to follow and the finished tank is adorable! The long flowing knit flatters all body types and the straps are wide enough to cover straps. This is the perfect tank pattern for anyone who is new to crochet; once you finish this top, you will want to start another one in a new color.

Skill Level: Easy

Materials: Sport weight yarn any color 5 balls or skeins. Hook U.S. size F and I. Yarn needle. Stitch markers.

Note on Sizes: This pattern makes sizes small, medium, large, 1x, and 2x. The pattern is for a size small, changes for larger sizes are in parentheses. Mark the changes for your size before beginning the pattern.

Size References: Bust Size: 32in. (36, 40, 44, 48) in.   Length: 27 ½ in. (29, 30 ½, 32 ½, 34) in.

Pattern

Band: Using the I hook, ch 26 (28, 31, 33, 36)

Row 1: hdc in the 3rd ch from the hook and in every ch across. 24, (26, 29, 31, 34) hdc. ch 2 then turn the project.

Row 2: hdc in every stitch across. Now repeat the last row until it measures, 33 in., (37, 41, 45, 49) in. from the beginning. Tie off the end. Now overlap the ends of the band by 1 in. then pin it to make the center back. Sew one long edge of the overlapped band to secure both layers together. The overlapped section is the back center, and bodice stitches will be done around the joined edge.

Bodice: With the RS facing, using the I hook, join the yarn with a sl st at the center back.

Rnd 1: ch2, now hdc 122, (138, 154, 170, 186) around the bottom of the band then join with a sl st in the first hdc.

Rnds 2-4: ch 2, then hdc in every stitch around and join with a sl st in first hdc of the round. Now change to the F hook and repeat the last round until the circumference measures 13 in. (14, 15, 16, 17) in. then tie off.

Straps: Measure 6in, (6, 6 ½, 6 ½, 7) in. across the top of the front edge of the band and mark it as the center.

Right Strap: With the RS facing, use the I hook and with a sl st attach the yarn on the left side of the marked center.

Row 1: ch 2 and hdc 13, (15, 15, 18, 18) across 3 in. (3 ½, 3 ½, 4, 4) in. toward the edge of the band. Then ch 2 and turn.

Row 2: hdc in every stitch across. Now repeat the last row until the strap measures, 18 in, (18, 18, 19, 19) in. Then tie off.

Left Strap: With the RS facing, use the I hook and with a sl st attach yarn 3 in. (3 ½, 3 ½, 4, 4) in. to the right of the marked center.

Row 1: ch 2 and hdc 13, (15, 15, 18, 18,) across to the marked section. ch 2 and turn.

Row 2: hdc in every stitch across. Now repeat the last row until the strap measures, 18, (18, 18, 19, 19) in. Now tie off.

Finish off by sewing the straps to the back band 5 in. (5, 5 ½, 5 ½, 6) in. from the center.

Chapter 3 – Cool Mesh Tank

The openwork crochet on this awesome tank makes it perfect for layering. This one looks good as a cover up too, just add several rows to the last row until it is the length you want. The cool mesh tank top is great over a contrasting color tank and paired with any bottom you love. The easy netting matches any style and this one is easy to personalize too. Just add a few crochet embellishments and you have a one of a kind tank top that will keep your wardrobe fresh and fun.

Skill Level: Intermediate

Materials: Sport weight yarn 5 balls or skeins any color, hook size G

Note on Sizes: This pattern makes sizes small, medium, large, 1x, and 2x. The pattern is for a size small, changes for larger sizes are in parentheses. Mark the changes for your size before beginning the pattern.

Pattern:

Front: Ch 91 (103, 115, 127, 139)

Row 1: 1 sc in the 7th ch, * ch 5 then skip 5 st, sc 1 in the next ch (this is one loop) *, repeat from * - * there should be 15 (17-19-21-23) loops, turn the work.

Row 2: ch 6, sc 1 in the first loop, * ch 5, sc 1 in the next loop *, repeat from * - * across the entire row then turn the work. Repeat Row 2 until the piece measures 6 in. Then inc 1 loop at each side = 17 (19, 21, 23, 25) loops.

Armhole: When the piece measures 13 in. (14, 15, 16, 17) in. crochet a binding for your size:

Size Small and Medium: Crochet until the last loop then turn the work, sl st to the center of the 1st loop, continue with the loops and repeat the binding on the other side.

Size Large and 1x: Follow the binding for size small and medium 1 time then turn the piece and crochet back to the last loop, turn the work again and continue with the loops and repeat the binding on the other side

Size 2x: Follow binding for size small and medium 2 times

Now there is a binding of 2 (2, 3, 3, 4) loops at each side. 13 (15, 15, 17, 17) loops remain on row. Repeat Row 2 again until the piece measures 14 ½ in. (15 ½, 16, 17, 18) in.

Neck: Crochet a binding for the neck, crochet 4 loops then turn the work and sl st to the center of first loop. Continue with loops until there are 3 loops on the shoulder. Repeat Row 2 again until the piece measures 20 in. (20 ½, 21 ½, 22, 23) in. Repeat on the other side of the neck.

Back: Crochet the same as the front. Crochet binding for armholes as on front. When the piece measures 19 in. (20, 20 ½, 21 ½, 22) in. crochet a binding for the neck by crocheting 2 rows over 3 loops on each shoulder, do not crochet over the center loops. The piece now measures approx. 20 in. (20 ½, 21 ½, 22, 23) in. tie off and the cut yarn.

Assembly: Crochet the shoulders together: 1 sl st in the first loop on the back, ch 3, 1 sc in the first loop on the front, ch 3, 1 sc in the next ch-loop on back, continue until complete. Now crochet the sides together the same way.

Neckband and Armhole Assembly: Crochet 1 row of hdc around the neck and both armholes as follows: * 1 hdc in sc, 2 hdc in loop *, repeat from * - * and finish with 1 sl st in first hdc on the row.

Chapter 4 – Easy Tunic Tank

This flattering tank top is the perfect length and it works worn over a top with sleeves or alone. The empire bodice design is flattering on all figures. The empire bodice is worked with a different stitch, giving the finished piece a stylish look without adding embellishments. This tank can be worn alone or layered and it is a perfect look for maxi skirts.

Skill Level: Easy/Intermediate

Materials: Sport weight yarn 5 balls or skeins any color, stitch markers, and plastic or metal yarn needle.

Hooks: For Bodice- US 7 and US 5. For the skirting- US 8 and US 9.

Note on Sizes: This pattern makes sizes small, medium, large, 1x, 2x, and 3x. The pattern is for a size small, changes for larger sizes are in parentheses. Mark the changes for your size before beginning the pattern.

Size References: Finished size for bust is, 31½ in. (35½, 39½, 43½, 47½, 49½) in. Finished size for the length is, 23½ in. (24¾, 25, 25, 26, 26½) in.

Instructions for Special Stitch:

Front post double crochet- abbreviation- FPdc

Yo and insert the hook behind the appropriate "post", the post is the straight part of a sc, dc, or any other basic crochet stitch. Yo and draw yarn through, [yo, draw yarn through 2 loops on hook], 2 times. Now you will skip the stitch behind the FPdc you just made.

Front Post
Fpdc = Front post dc

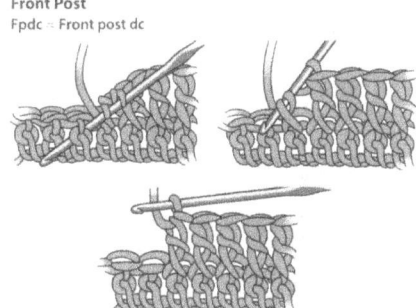

Notes: The bodice is worked from bottom to top in two separate pieces and attached with a seam. For the rest of the tank, stitches are picked up on the opposite side of the fabric and worked in the round from the waist to the hem.

Pattern:

Back of Bodice: Using crochet hook 5, ch 64 (72, 80, 88, 96, 108)

Row 1: sc in the second chain from the hook, and in every chain across. Turn, sc 63 (71, 79, 87, 95, 107).

Row 2: RS facing, ch1, now sc in every stitch across. Turn.

Row 3: Repeat row 2

Row 4: ch 1, sc in the first 3 sc. *FPdc in next sc 2 rows below, sc in the next 3 stitches, repeat from * across then turn.

Row 5: Repeat row 2

Row 6: ch 1 then sc in the first 3 stitches. Now *FPdc in the next sc 2 rows below**. sc in the next 3 sc, repeat from * across and end the last repeat at **, sc in the last sc then turn.

Now repeat rows 3-6 until you have 15 (15, 15, 15, 17, 17) rows are complete. Make adjustments if needed to keep the FPdc stitches in alingment with each other.

Arm Hole Right Side:

Row 1: sl st across 4 (5, 5, 6, 7, 8) sts, ch 1 then maintain the stitch pattern, continue until you reach the last 4 (5, 5, 6, 7, 8) sts. Turn, leave the remaining sts unworked—55 (61. 69. 75, 81, 91) sts.

Row 2: ch 1 and skip the first stitch, now continue across until you reach the last 2 sts. Sc in the last st then turn--53 (59, 67, 73, 79, 89) sts.

Row 3: Repeat row 2, (5, 7, 9, 11,16) 5 times--43 (49, 53, 55, 57, 57) sts.

Work the estabished pattern until you have 32 (32, 34, 34, 34, 34) rows from the beginning of the armhole.

First Shoulder:

Row 1 (right side): ch 1 and work in the established pattern across 17 (19, 20, 20, 20, 20) sts, turn and leave the remaining sts unworked-- 17 (19, 20, 20, 20, 20)

Row 2: sl st across the first 5 sts, ch 1 then work in pattern across, then turn--12 (14, 15, 15, 15, 15) sts.

Row 3: ch 1 then work in pattern across to the last 2 sts, skip the next st and sc in the last st then turn—11 (13, 14, 14, 14, 14) sts.

Row 4: ch 1 then skip the next st, work in pattern across then turn-- 10 (12, 13, 13, 13, 13) sts.

Repeat rows 3 and 4 two more times-- 6 (8, 9, 9, 9, 9) sts.

Work the established pattern until you have completed 44 (46, 48, 50, 50, 52) rows from the beginning of the armhole then tie off.

Second Shoulder:

Row 1 (right side): with the right side facing, skip 9 (11, 13, 15, 17, 17) sts to the left of the last st in row 1 of the first shoulder. Now ch 1 and starting in the same st, work the pattern across then turn--17 (19, 20, 20, 20, 20) sts.

Row 2: ch 1 then work pattern across until the last 5 sts then turn and leave the remaining sts unworked-- 12 (14, 15, 15, 15, 15) sts.

Row 3: ch 1 then skip the first st, work the pattern across, turn-- 11 (13, 14, 14, 14, 14) sts.

Row 4: ch 1, now work pattern across until you reach the last 2 sts, skip the next st, sc in the last st then turn-- 10 (12, 13, 13, 13, 13) sts.

Repeat rows 3 and 4 two more times-- 6 (8, 9, 9, 9, 9) sts.

Work the established pattern until you have completed 44 (46, 48, 50, 50, 52) rows from the beginning of the armhole then tie off.

Bodice Front: Work the same as you did for the back of the bodice until you have 28 (28, 30, 30, 30, 30) rows completed from the beginning of the armhole.

Next Row (right side): ch 1 then work in pattern across the first 11 (13, 14, 14, 14, 14) sts, turn and leave the remaining sts unworked-- 11 (13, 14, 14, 14, 14) sts.

Next Row: ch 1 then skip the first st, work pattern across then turn-- 10 (12, 13, 13, 13, 13) sts

Nex Row: ch 1 then work pattern across until you reach the last 2 sts, skip the next st, sc in the last st, now turn-- 9 (11, 12, 12, 12, 12) sts.

Repeat the last 2 rows once-- 7 (9, 10, 10, 10, 10) sts.

Next Row: ch 1 then skip the next st, now work the pattern across then turn - 6 (8, 9, 9, 9, 9) sts.

Work the pattern until you have completed 44 (46, 48, 50, 50, 52) rows from the beginning of the armhole then tie off.

Second Shoulder:

Row 1: With the right side facing, skip 21 (23, 25, 27, 29, 29) sts to the left of the last st made in row 1 of the first shoulder. Ch 1, starting in the same st, work the pattern across, turn-- 11 (13, 14, 14, 14, 14) sts.

Row 2: ch 1, work the pattern across until you reach the last 2 sts, skip the next st, sc ch in last st then turn-- 10 (12, 13, 13, 13, 13) sts.

Row 3: ch 1, skip the first st, work the pattern across then turn, 9 (11, 12, 12, 12, 12) sts.

Repeat rows 2 and 3 two times-- 7 (9, 10, 10, 10, 10) sts.

Repeat row 2 one time-- 6 (8, 9, 9, 9, 9) sts.

Work the pattern until you have completed 44 (46, 48, 50, 50, 52) rows from the beginning of the armhole, then tie off.

Assemble the Bodice: Using the yarn needle, whipstitch the side and shoulder seams.

Armhole Trim:

Round 1: Right side facing, use the 7 hook and start at the bottom of the armhole, ch 1, then sc around then sl st in the first ch to join.

Rounds 2, 3, and 4: ch 1 then sc in each sc around and join with a sl st in the first chain. Tie off after round 4.

Skirting (bottom of the tunic):

Round 1: Right side facing, using 9 hook, join with a sl st to the bottom back center of the bodice. Ch 1 and sc in every sc around then sl st in the first sc-- 126 (142, 158, 174, 190, 214) sts.

Round 2: ch 1 and sc in every sc around, work 14 (8, 6, 4, 4, 2) evenly spaced increases, then sl st in first sc to join-- 140 (150, 164, 178, 194, 216) sc.

Begin working in a spiral and sc without joining, continue until the skirt reaches 9 in. (10, 10, 10, 10, 10) in. from the begining of the skirt. Now end at the center back and sl st to join.

Next Round: Working with the 8 hook, ch 1 then sc in each sc around then sl st to join-- 140 (150, 164, 178, 196, 216) sc.

Repeat the last round until the skirt measures, 11½ in. (12½, 12½, 12½, 12½, 12½) in. from the beginning of the skirt. Now tie off and weave in the ends.

Chapter 5 – Sweet Shell Stitch Tank

Skill Level: Intermediate

Materials: Sport or worsted weight yarn 5 balls or skeins any color, hook size US G and a yarn needle.

Note on Sizes: This pattern makes sizes x-small, small, medium, large, x-large. The pattern is for a size x-small, changes for larger sizes are in parentheses. Mark the changes for your size before beginning the pattern.

Finished Sizes: Finished bust- 25 ½ in. (28, 30 ½, 32 ½, 35) in. Back length- 20 ½ in. (20 ½, 20 ½, 21 ¼, 21 ¼) in.

Note for Special Stitch: This tank top uses the shell stitch. The shell stitch is created by making 5 dc in on stitch.

Pattern:

Back of Tank: Ch 68 (74, 80, 86, 92)

Row 1 (right side): sc in the second ch from the hook, skip the next 2 chs, then shell in the next ch, skip the next 2 chs, sc in the next ch, repeat across 11 [12, 13, 14, 15] shells then turn.

Row 2 (wrong side): ch 3, 2 dc in the first sc, sc in center of the dc of the next shell, shell in the next sc, sc in the center dc of the next shell, continue across until you reach the last sc, now 3 dc in the last sc--10 (11, 12, 13, 14 shells and 2 half shells) now turn.

Row 3: ch 1 then sc in the first dc, skip the next 2 dc, shell in the next sc, sc in the center dc of the next shell, now repeat across until you reach the last sc, shell in the next sc, skip the next 2 dc, sc in the last dc--11 (12, 13, 14, 15) shells.

Repeat rows 2 and 3 until the piece measures 11 ½ in. and be sure to end with row 2.

Back Armholes: With right side facing, sl st to the center dc of the first (first, first, second, second) shell, ch 1, sc in dc, work the pattern across until you reach the last shell. Sc in the dc of shell 9 (10, 11, 10, 11), now turn and leave the remaining sts unworked.

Work in this established pattern for 13 (13, 13, 15, 15) rows.

Back Right Neck:

Row 1: With the right side facing, ch 1, sc in the first dc then shell stitch in the next sc. Sc in the center of the dc in the shell then complete 3 more shell stitches. Now turn the work and leave the remaining stitches unworked.

Row 2: sl st to the center of the dc in the first shell then ch 1 and sc in dc, now shell the next sc. Work this pattern across to the last sc, 3 dc in the last sc, (2 shell and a half shell), now turn.

Row 3: ch 1, sc in the first dc, now shell in the next sc, sc in the center of the next shell and repeat 1 time (2 shells) turn and leave the remaining stitches unworked.

Work this pattern for 4 rows then tie off.

Back Left Neck:

Row 1: With right side facing, skip center 2 (3, 4, 3, 4) shells then skip the next sc and join the yarn in the center dc of the next shell. Ch 1 then sc in dc, now work the pattern across (3 shells) now turn.

Row 2: ch 3 (first dc), now 2 dc in the first sc, work the pattern across to the last shell then sc in the center of the dc of the last shell (2 shells and half shell), leave the remaining stitches unworked and turn.

Row 3: sl st to the center dc of the first shell then ch1 and sc in dc. Work the pattern across (2 shells), now turn the work.

Front Piece:

Ch 68 (74, 80, 86, 92)

Row 1 (right side): sc in the second ch from the hook, skip the nex 2 chs then shell in the next 2 chs, sc in the next ch then repeat across (11 [12, 13, 14, 15] shells and 2 half shells) now turn.

Row 2 (wrong side): ch 3 (the first dc) now 2 dc in the first sc (half shell made), sc in the center dc of the next shell and shell in the next sc. Now sc in the center dc of the next shell and repeat across to the last sc, 3 dc in the last sc (10 [11, 12, 13, 14] shells and 2 half shells), now turn.

Row 3: ch 1 then sc in the first dc, now skip the next 2 dc, shell in the next sc, sc in the center dc of the next shell, now repeat across to the last sc, shell in the last sc then skip the next 2 dc and sc in the last dc (11 [12, 13, 14, 15] shells), now turn.

Repeat rows 2-3 until the front piece measures 11 ½ in. from the beginning. End with a Row 2.

Front Armholes

Row 1 (right side): sl st to the center dc of the 1st (1st, 1st, 2nd, 2nd) shell and ch 1, then sc in dc and work the pattern across to the last 1 (1, 1, 2, 2) shells. Now sc in the center dc of shell (9 [10, 11, 10, 11] shells), now turn and leave the remaining stitches unworked.

Work the pattern for 3 more rows.

Front Left Neck:

Row 1 (right side): ch 1 the sc in the first dc and shell in the next sc, sc in the center dc of the next shell, repeat 2 times (3 shells), turn and leave the remaining stitches unworked.

Row 2: sl st to the center of the dc of the first shell, now ch 1 and sc in dc, shell in the next sc and work the pattern across to the last sc, 3 dc in the last sc (2 shells and a half shell), turn the work.

Row 3: ch 1 and sc in the first dc, shell in the next sc and sc in the center dc of the next shell, repeat once (2 shells), now turn and leave the remaining stitches unworked.

Work the pattern for 14 (14, 14, 16, 16) more rows and then tie off.

Right Neck:

Row 1: with the right side facing, skip the center 2 (3, 4, 3, 4) shells then skip the next sc, now join the yarn in the center dc of the next shell, ch 1 and sc in dc, now work the pattern across (3 shells) and turn.

Row 2: ch 2 (first dc) and 2 dc in the first sc, now work the pattern across to the last shell, then sc in the center dc of the last shell (2 shells and a half shell), now turn and leave the remaining stitches unworked.

Row 3: sl st to the center dc of the first shell and ch 1, then sc in dc and work pattern across (2 shells), turn the work.

Work the established pattern for 14 (14, 14, 16, 16) more rows then tie off.

Assemble:

With the right sides facing, use the yarn needle and yarn to sew the front to the back across the shoulders with a whip stitch.

At the lower edge of each side, match stitches across the side edges and sew the side seams from the edge to the armholes.

With the right sides facing, join the yarn in the side seam at the lower edge of one armhole, ch1 the sc around the entire armhole then sl st in the first sc to join, now tie off.

Repeat the armhole edge around the other armhole.

Conclusion

Now you have a few editions for you summer wardrobe and these tanks go with everything. The skills you have picked up for creating these tank tops will take you into your next project and beyond! Each pattern is unique and you can dress them up or down, add extra rows at the bottom to create a tank dress or loose a few rows at the bottom for a crop tank.

The cleaning and care of your new garments depends on the yarn you choose. Always follow the manufacturer's instructions for washing, this is located on the wrap around the yarn. Some yarns like sport yarn are easy care, wools may need dry cleaning. Your new tank tops must be folded and stored, never hang them by the shoulders; the yarn makes the item a bit heavy and it will stretch out of shape.

Just think! Now you have the skills and the patterns to dress yourself and anyone else in style. It is time to learn a bit of embellishing skill so you can dress up those one of a kind tanks and make a fashion statement on the beach, boardwalk, or out on the town.